A JOURNEY INTO LOVE

A JOURNEY INTO LOVE

MEDITATING WITH THE
MEDIEVAL POEM *PIERS PLOWMAN*

Mary Clemente Davlin, O. P.

MARYMOUNT
INSTITUTE PRESS

LOS ANGELES | NEW YORK | OXFORD | PRETORIA | ADDIS ABABA

Printed in the United States of America

MARYMOUNT
INSTITUTE PRESS

A Journey into Love: Meditating with the Medieval Poem Piers Plowman
Copyright © 2008 by Mary Clemente Davlin, O. P. All rights reserved.

Tsehai books may be purchased for educational, business, or sales promotional use. For more information, please contact our special sales department.

Marymount Institute Press, a Tsehai Publishers imprint
Loyola Marymount University
One LMU Drive, Suite 3012 | Los Angeles, CA 90045

www.tsehaipublishers.com/mip
eMail: mip@tsehaipublishers.com

Editor: Theresia de Vroom | Publisher: Elias Wondimu
Copy edited by Yalemzewd Worku | Layout and cover design by Evguenl Groisman
Photography by Stephen Shepherd | Cover art by Will Pupa

First Edition, March 2008

ISBN: 978-1-59907-031-5

Library of Congress Catalog Card Number
A catalog record for this book is available from the Library of Congress.

British Library Cataloguing in Publication Data.
A catalogue record for this book is available from the British Library.

10 9 8 7 6 5 4 3 2 1

The Robert B. Lawton S.J. Studies in Faith, Culture, and the Arts is published by the Marymount Institute Press at Loyola Marymount University in Los Angeles, California. The series publishes books that cross disciplines and genres and explore the interdisciplinary and intercultural dialogue between faith, art, culture, religion, literature, music, language, history, film, and science.

TABLE OF CONTENTS

CONTENTS

LIST OF ILLUSTRATIONS

ILLUSTRATIONS

All photographs are of the West Country and the Southwest Midlands of England, a region in which it is generally agreed that Langland grew up. The Malvern Hills in this region provide the setting for the opening of the poem. It is possible that the cathedrals depicted in these photographs were visited by Langland himself.

PREFACE

The words of the poet William Plowden were perhaps never better suited than to describe the making of this book: "the ripest fruit hangs where not one but only two can reach." The publication of *The Journey into Love*, however, is a result of the labor of many more people than two. This book first came to our attention when Sr. Mary Clemente Davlin, O.P. participated in a mini-conference organized by my colleague, Stephen Shepherd, called *Time Past in Time Present: The Relevance of Pre-Modernity*. Stephen, himself a scholar and editor of *Piers Plowman*, is also and coincidentally the photographer of all the images inside this book—suffice it to say that he has been an invaluable help and support on a variety of levels in the process of bringing this book to print. The four scholars who gathered together one night last October in the Marymount Institute at Loyola Marymount University did so in order to answer the basic question: why teach old things? And in particular, why teach *Piers Plowman* today? Of the many remarkable arguments proposed by the scholars, artists, and students in attendance, came Sr. Mary Clemente Davlin's dazzling meditation on the poem for contemporary readers contained herein. It is her vision, breadth and profound understanding of the poem that illuminates the fourteenth century in the twenty-first and captures the human struggle to live justly and well across the span of time, spirituality and culture.

In a time when the publishing of books is routinely controlled by multinational corporations, the birth of a small press is a rare and significant event. I first met Elias Wondimu one year ago to date. A publisher, activist, and journalist in exile from his native Ethiopia, Elias has been the driving force behind the creation of the Marymount Institute Press. Working in collaboration with Elias has been a true labor of love: the love of books that matter and the rare and deeply human joy of working together to make public and accessible works of artistic beauty and intellectual complexity.

I also wish to acknowledge and thank Will Pupa, artist–in–residence for the Marymount Institute, for his extraordinary cover drawing, "The hand of God holds the world" which is modeled on the original fifteenth-century drawing found in a manuscript of the poem. I want to thank Ernie Rose, CAO, for his unwavering support of the Institute. And finally, I wish to thank Lane Bove, Senior Vice President for Student Affairs and Chair of the Advisory Board for the Marymount Institute for Faith, Culture and the Arts without whose guidance the Marymount Institute Press would not have been possible.

This is the first book published by the Marymount Institute Press and it is the first in a series fittingly named for our LMU President, Robert B. Lawton, S.J., a man who has devoted his life to the dialogue between faith, culture and the arts. Trained in Classics and Near Eastern Languages and Civilizations, Fr. Lawton also presides over a campus that overlooks the diverse, vibrant, and post-modern city of Los Angeles. He is the living embodiment of the efficacy and value of the study of a past that can know, understand, and shape the present. It is in the spirit of his far-ranging intellect and his expansive grace that we dedicate the Robert B. Lawton Studies in Faith, Culture, and the Arts.

Theresia de Vroom
Director of the Marymount Institute for Faith, Culture and the Arts
Professor of English
Loyola Marymount University

AUTHOR'S ACKNOWLEDGEMENTS

Generations of scholars and editors of *Piers Plowman* have made this poem accessible to us. Personally, I thank especially Mary Paynter, O.P., who introduced me first to *Piers* and who devised the title for this book; Professor Charles Muscatine, who guided me as I began to study it and has helped and inspired me ever since; Jeanne Crapo, O.P., the late Mary Brian Durkin, O.P., and Ellen McManus, who read and improved earlier versions of this text; my other Dominican Sisters, who have made my years of study possible; all those students, colleagues, and others who have shared their love for the poem with me; Theresia de Vroom for her expert editing and collaboration; Stephen Shepherd, whose photos adorn these pages, for his art and generosity; Will Pupa for his contemporary version of the medieval hand of God; Elias Wondimu for his expertise; and the Marymount Institute Press for making this text available to those for whom it was written.

INTRODUCTION

Piers Plowman is the best-kept secret in religious and spiritual literature.

Written in the late fourteenth century, at about the same time Chaucer was writing his *Canterbury Tales* and just after the Black Plague swept across Europe, *Piers* is well-known and valued by students of English literature, but almost unknown among those for whom it was probably written—people interested in living better lives.

This book is intended for them. It contains selections and brief commentary designed to give the reader a "taste" of the poem, its nourishing power and its extraordinary beauty.

Piers Plowman is a work of fiction, a book-length poem about a man named Will who goes out seeking adventure. As he wanders, he falls asleep and has a series of ten dreams in which, arguing with the people he dreams about and listening to their debates, he learns about himself, his world, and God. The character for whom the poem is named, Piers the Plowman (Piers is a form of "Peter"), is a mysterious and attractive figure who appears in Will's dreams several times. A poor laborer, he has come to know God intimately and is willing to teach others how to do so.

Will comes to love and follow Piers, whose identity gradually becomes more mysterious.

Throughout the narrative, Will is looking for an understanding of God, of life and of himself. He wanders and dreams until he grows old, and as he faces old age, he realizes that his society is becoming corrupt. The poem ends with a new search for Piers to save society. It dramatizes the spiritual journey of every human being as an individual and as a member of society, the mistakes we make, our hopes, despairs, and follies, and the wonderful kindness of God in searching us out. The poem's sense of God is of a mysterious Being infinitely good and loving, who journeys through the universe seeking to share the sorrows of humanity and to bring us to joy.

But the delight of the book is not limited to its story. Some other reasons for its attractiveness to people of our time are its affirmation of the body, sexuality, nature, marriage, and family, its emphasis upon the need for social justice, its vivid representation of poverty and the clarity of its ethical theory, centered on love. Neither romantic nor unduly idealistic, *Piers Plowman* is a hopeful poem in which the promise of salvation is extended to every person. It is an experiential poem, shaped by the human experiences of poverty, sin and folly, forgiveness, aging, love, and work. In ways that we can accept today, the poem presents women and men as equal and ponders the nature of a God whose all-encompassing being the poem calls by gender-inclusive names such as "Truth," "Nature," and "Love."

Piers is a work of extreme beauty, written in a form of poetry almost unknown now, the alliterative line. It is filled with vivid images and compelling sounds. Alliterative poetry does not rhyme. It is rhythmic, and its music comes from the repetition of a consonant sound several times in each line, like "s" in the first line: "In a summer season, when the sun was soft."

Piers Plowman is a work of deep wisdom, based on an unusually profound understanding of the Bible, the liturgy of the Church, and the writings of the Church fathers. The scholar Morton Bloomfield once said that the author "speaks Bible," and indeed Bible readers will find themselves at home in this poem which quotes both Hebrew and Christian scriptures every few lines. Those who have not read the Bible may be drawn to it by the various—sometimes conflicting—interpretations that are sometimes sublime, sometimes earthy, humorous, and poignant. At the same time, the poem is steeped in Christian liturgy. It explores the experience of sacramental life and of the festivals of the Church year, especially the Easter season and Pentecost.

Although it is over six hundred years old, *Piers Plowman* seems peculiarly fitted to the twenty-first century. Still, the poem has been relatively inaccessible to anyone except academics. The time has come to make the poem available to the audience for which it was originally written, ordinary people, and it is my hope that this is what this book will do.

Piers Plowman is straightforward yet invitingly complex. It is an allegorical work, which is to say that much of its action takes place in Will's mind, and many of the characters he meets have names that represent them like "Wit," "Holy Church," and "Nature." Unlike many of the simpler emotional religious lyrics of its time, this poem seeks to explore the great mysteries of Christianity as objects of faith and sources of love. It attempts to bring the reader into an experience of mysteries such as the Trinity, the Incarnation, and the indwelling, without oversimplifying them. Its style is rich and strong, its tones are encyclopedic, ranging from farce to ecstasy, from common sense to mystery. It holds something for everyone; one can think about it endlessly without tiring of it.

This book is an invitation and an introduction to *Piers Plowman*, which seems to have been written to help readers deepen their faith and experience of the Divine. It is a masterpiece of our heritage, a pre-Reformation Christian poem (belonging therefore to both Catholics and Protestants, since it comes from the time when they had not separated) which praises Jews and argues for the salvation of unbelievers.

There is already a wealth of scholarly literature that analyzes the structure of the whole poem, the order and meaning of its parts, the interpretation of its characters and passages. Here, I want to present in Modern English a few of its passages with a brief commentary to demonstrate a little of the poem's spirituality and the brilliance of its language. The best way to read these passages is slowly, in any order you find attractive and in small "bites," savoring the ones which appeal to you. I would encourage those who enjoy these passages to go on to read a whole translation (of which some are listed at the end of this volume), and then, perhaps, to read their favorite passages or the entire poem in the original Middle English, with the help of some books and articles also listed at the end.

The translation or modernization given here is my own. It is inevitable that it will overlap with or depend upon translations by others in part and occasionally coincide with earlier translations. Sometimes this is because both translations follow the original Middle English text closely with only the spelling modernized; I have not listed coincidences of this kind. However, at the end of the volume, I have cited all conscious borrowings and lengthy coincidences.

We know very little about the author of *Piers Plowman* except that he lived and wrote in the West Midlands of England (near Hereford, Gloucester, and Worcester) and in London at the end of the fourteenth century. He has his main character in the poem say, "My name is Will; I have lived long in the land," and because scholars think that this may have been the sort of "signature" common at that time, the author has been called William Langland, though that may not have been his name. He speaks of monastery schools with affection, so he may have had a Benedictine education through what we would call secondary school. There is no evidence of a William Langland attending university. He knew Latin and had a profound understanding of the Bible and the prayers of the church. His main character (and perhaps he himself) was married to "Kitte" and had a daughter named "Calote." In the poem, Will says that he earns his living by singing prayers for the dead, and writes because only by writing can he understand how to live. Langland seems to have spent his entire adult life writing and revising this one poem.

The author of *Piers Plowman* is not only one of our greatest poets, but also one of the greatest spiritual teachers in the English language. May his words help you in your journey into love.

How the Story Begins

As the poem begins, Will, the speaker, tells us how he starts on a summer journey in search of "wonders," but goes to sleep. His first dream is of the whole world: a high tower in the east, which suggests heaven; a dark dungeon, which suggests hell; and a whole world of people in between. Thus, the poem begins as it will end, with a vision of society. But the vision is mysterious, and Will does not understand it.

In a summer season, when the sun was soft,

I dressed in a sheep's clothing,

. . . like a hermit unholy of works,

And went far in this world to hear wonders.

But on a May morning on Malvern hills,

A wonder befell me, an enchantment, I thought.

I was weary from wandering, and went to rest

Under a broad hill by a stream's side,

And as I lay and leaned and looked on the waters,

I slumbered into sleep, it sounded so merry.

Then I dreamed a marvelous dream—

That I was in a wilderness, I never knew where.

As I looked into the east, high up to the sun,

I saw a tower on a hill, beautifully made,

A deep dale beneath it with a dungeon in it,

With deep ditches and dark, and dreadful to see.

A fair field full of folk I found between—

Of all manner of people, the poor and the rich

Working and wandering as the world requires.

   (Pro. 1-19)

Truth

Often in the poem, when Will needs assistance, someone turns up to help him. The first helper is a lady, beautiful but a little intimidating, who says she is "Lady Holy Church." She proceeds to explain that Truth, who lives in the tower, is the Creator, and that Wrong, who lives in the dungeon, is the father of falsehood and leads people to turn away from love.

"Truth, true" are among the most important words in *Piers Plowman*, words meaning "fidelity, faithfulness, faithful" ("I will be true to you"), as well as (Aquinas's definition) "the conformity of the mind to reality" ("I tell the truth.") The poem uses "Truth" as a name for God.

Wrong, the father of falseness, urges people to betray, to disobey, to kill, and he betrays those who trust him. Truth is the opposite. He is faithful—true and trustworthy. One can count on Truth.

People live in between these two realities and choose between them.

"The tower on the hill," she said, "Truth is therein. . . .

He is the faithful father and formed you all

With skin and with face, and gave you five wits

To worship him with while you are here" . . .

"That dungeon in the dale, dreadful to see . . .

That is the castle of cares. Whoever enters there

May curse that he was born to body or to soul!

Therein lives a person called Wrong,

Father of falseness, [who] founded it himself.

Adam and Eve he egged on to evil,

Counseled Cain to kill his brother."

    (1. 12, 14-16, 59, 61-66)

In the poem, "truth" is also the name for an important human quality.

Notice that it includes honesty, veracity, and also love that "wills no one evil".

"When all treasures are tried," she said,

"Truth is the best.

I base it on *'God is love,'* to tell the truth.

It is as precious a treasure as dear God himself.

For whoever is true of tongue and tells no lies

And does the works of truth and wills no one evil,

Is a god by the gospel, on earth and above,

And like to our Lord, by St. Luke's words."

      (1. 79—91)

How is truth, both as honest accuracy and as faithfulness, important in your relationships?

What do you think it means that truth is as precious a treasure as God?

Look at some of the "definitions" of truth which Will is given in the next few pages. Why is it such a precious treasure?

Truth is also a faithful steadfastness in doing good and avoiding evil.

To do no deadly sin, even if you should have to die—

This I believe is truth . . .

    (1. 144-5)

Can you think of a person who is true in this sense?

Using truth as a name both for human goodness and for the Divine suggests that truth somehow *relates* us to God or makes us like God. Thus, those that "end . . . in truth" will "go to heaven / Where Truth is." They have *become* true and will always be where Truth, the best treasure, is.

Those that work well as Holy Writ says

And end, as I said before, in truth, that is the best,

May be sure that their souls shall go to heaven

Where Truth is in Trinity and enthrones them all.

    (1. 130—133)

In what ways can people be Godlike?

Love

"Love," or charity, is another important word in the poem. It is used as "truth" is, both for a human quality and as a name for God.

Love, which includes truth, is the chief virtue. It is not simply a feeling, but a firm, loyal will to "do good against evil." It is also "docile as a good child," cheerful, "friendly and comforting."

For charity is God's champion, and docile as a good child,

And the merriest of speech where he sits at table.

The love that lies in his heart makes him light of speech,

And friendly and comforting, as Christ bade himself.

    (15. 216—19)

Try to imagine or remember a person who is "love." What is such a person like?

The poet agrees with St. Paul that no other virtue is of value unless it is suffused with love. "Chastity without charity," he says, is an evil thing which "will be chained in hell," since it has "no light" in it.

For even if you be true of your tongue and earn [your living] honestly

And as chaste as a child that weeps in church,

Unless you love loyally and give to the poor

[and] share well such goods as God has sent you,

You have no more merit in mass or in prayers

Than Malkyn has of her maidenhead that no man desires. . .

Therefore, chastity without charity will be chained in hell;

It is as blind as a lamp that no light is in.

    (1.179—84, 188—9)

Do you agree? What would justice be like without love? Honesty? Courage? Cleverness?

Holy Church describes love also as the medicine or salve of heaven. The Middle English word translated here as "medicine" is really "*triacle*"—a kind of herbal remedy still sold as a molasses candy ("treacle toffee.") Using love, "that spice," she says, removes the poison of sin from a person's life.

For Truth tells that love is the medicine of heaven;

No sin may be seen on one who uses that spice.

    (1. 148—9)

Has love ever been a salve or medicine in your life?

Holy Church says that love is the "plant of peace." She tells Will that God, who is Love, came down from heaven, and like a seed falling into the ground, took earth (flesh and blood) from Mary's body. Holy Church compares the child that is born from the seed to a tree commonly found in Britain, the linden or lime tree, which has medicinal and healing properties.

And [love is] also the plant of peace, most precious of virtues;

For heaven might not hold it, it was so heavy in itself

Until it had eaten its fill of earth.

And when it had taken flesh and blood of this earth,

There was never leaf on a linden lighter thereafter

And portable and piercing as the point of a needle,

So no armor could resist it, nor any high walls [keep it out].

    (1. 152—8)

What do you think it means that "heaven could not hold" love because it was so heavy?

What do you think Lady Holy Church means when she says that love, human as well as divine, is portable and piercing as a needle?

In your experience, can anything keep love out?

Where does love come from? How does one come to know it? Holy Church says its source is in the heart, and she gives the example of the love of God. Out of love, the Father let his Son die for us, and Jesus "granted mercy / To them that hung him high and pierced his heart." He "was mighty and meek"—he showed his power, not by punishing, but by forgiving.

Holy Church says that we must do the same by having pity on others' misfortunes and by sharing with them. She challenges the rich and privileged, even though they have power in the courts over the poor, to be merciful and loving, as they hope to obtain mercy from God.

And in the heart, there is the source and the deep fountain.

For in deep knowledge in the heart there comes a power—

And that is related to the Father that formed us all,

Looked on us with love, and let his son die

Meekly for our misdeeds, to amend us all.

And yet he [Jesus] wished no evil on them that caused him that pain . .

. . . he was mighty and meek, and granted mercy

To them that hung him high and pierced his heart.

Therefore I advise you rich, have pity on the poor,

Even if you are mighty enough to take them to court, be meek in your works,

For the same measure that you mete out . . .

You shall be weighed with when you go hence.

(1. 164—9, 173—8)

Where do you find love in your own life?

For this poet, love must be loyal, faithful, and constant. And the power of love is to make us act like "blood relatives," even with those who do evil against us.

Be sure that you love loyally, if you want to do well . . .

   (10. 189)

[Theology] bids us to be as blood relatives and pray for our enemies,

And love those that lie about us, and give to them when they have need,

And do good against evil.

   (10. 199—201)

What would it mean if all human beings could view each other as "blood relatives"—related by ties of family and kinship? Can you think of someone or some group of people you distrust or fear whom you would see differently if you were related?

Giving is "the lock of love that lets out my grace." *Lock* here may mean "something that holds a door shut or allows it to open," but it may also mean "the lock of a river, letting the water flow." The second meaning seems to fit with the previous image of Christ's pierced heart, which let out water and blood.

We have already been told that love is medicine. Now Holy Church says that love is also the "physician of life" and that love is the thing "nearest to Our Lord himself."

At the end of this passage, Holy Church leaves Will.

Give, and it shall be given to you, for I take care of you all.

And that is the lock of love that lets out my grace

To comfort the worried, burdened with sin.

Love is the physician of life and next to Our Lord himself,

And also the road that goes directly to heaven.

Therefore I say as I said before, in the light of these texts,

When all treasures are tried, truth is the best.

Now I have told thee what truth is—that no treasure is better.

I may no longer linger with thee. Now our Lord look to thee!

    (Luke 6:38) (1. 201-9)

In what sense is love a "road that goes directly to heaven"?

Kynde

Another important word in this poem is the Middle English *kynde* (which rhymes with "leaned"). Like the modern word, "kind," it means several things— "species" and therefore "kin": ("humankind," "what kind of tree is that?" "he is kin to me"), "loving" ("she was very kind to me"); but it also means "nature" as a whole.

Kynde is also a name for God as the Creator of nature. The poet plays with these four meanings, connecting them, as we can see in these passages.

Philosophers and theologians in this period spoke of *natura naturans*—Nature the Creator of nature (that is, God)—as well as *natura naturata*—nature created by Nature (what we call "nature"). So although it seems strange to us, it wasn't unusual to call God "Nature" as the poet does here. And because of the several meanings of *kynde,* this name for God also has overtones of the divine kindness.

Kynde . . . is creator of all species of things,

Father and former of all that ever was made—

And that is the great God that never had beginning,

Lord of life and of light, of bliss and of pain.

    (9. 26-29)

What connections do you see between God and nature? Between God and kindness? Does it seem natural to you to be kind?

The "castle that *Kynde* made" is the human body, in which *Kynde* has "craftily enclosed" the human spirit whom he loves," and who is "like to himself."

"Sir Do Well dwells," said Wit, "not a day from here,

In a castle that *Kynde* made of four kinds of things.

Of earth and air it is made, mixed together

With wind and with water, wittily joined.

Kynde has craftily enclosed therein

A beloved whom he loves, like to himself.

She is called the Soul . . ."

    (9. 1—7)

What difference would it make if we thought of each other's bodies as architectural works made lovingly by God?

Kynde calls Will outdoors to observe the beauty of the world, the sun and the sea, the birds and the beasts, and "through each creature" to learn to love his Creator. Beside the sheer perfection of nature, however, human beings are revealed to be both good and bad; they engender both "poverty and plenty," "peace and war," "bliss and suffering."

. . . and then came *Kynde*

And named me by my name, and bade me take heed

And learn from the wonders of this world.

And on a mountain called Middle Earth,

I was brought out to learn from examples,

Through each creature, to love *Kynde*, my Creator.

I saw the sun and the sea and the sand after,

And where birds and beasts go with their mates,

Wild serpents in woods, and wonderful birds

With flecked feathers, and of many colors.

Man and his mate I could see,

Poverty and plenty, peace and war,

Bliss and suffering—both I saw at once,

And how people took graft and refused mercy.

(11.320-333)

How can one learn to love the Creator through nature?

What do you think it means to "refuse mercy"?

In some of the most beautiful nature poetry before the nineteenth century, Will marvels at the intricacy of *Kynde's* work. Here he illustrates one way to meditate, simply by looking at an animal, or bird, or fish, or star, a nest or some other aspect of nature, and marveling at its beauty and complexity.

Birds I beheld that in bushes made nests,

No human had the wit to work the littlest part of this.

I marveled from whom and where the magpie

Learned to lay the sticks in which she lies and breeds.

There is no carpenter, I think, who could make her nest so well;

If any mason made a mould of it, it would be a great wonder.

   (11.344-49)

And then I looked upon the sea and then upon the stars;

Many marvels I saw, too many to tell.

I saw flowers in the forest and their fair colors

And how among the green grass so many hues grew

And some sour and some sweet—marvelous, I thought:

It would take too long to talk of their kinds and their colors.

   (11. 362—7)

How does the natural world cause you to marvel?

Near the end of the poem, the Good Samaritan talks with Will and plays with the words *kynde, unkynde, kyndenesse, unkyndenesse.* Unkindness is the contrary of kindness, of course, and since, in this period, *kynde* also means "natural," to be unkind is to be unnatural or monstrous. *Unkyndenesse* is also the contrary of *Kynde,* the Spirit of God, God's own nature and kindness. Thus, deliberately hurting another person or destroying a human life is the undoing of creation, the undoing of what the Holy Spirit does and cares for.

The poet says that our unkindness to one another "quenches" God's grace by "undoing" the life or happiness of another who is the kind creation of God.

. . . [if you are] unkind to your kin,

The Holy Spirit does not hear you, nor can help you . . .

For unkindness quenches him so that he cannot shine

Nor burn, nor blaze clear, because of the blowing of unkindness.

    (17. 254—7)

Thus unkindness is the contrary, that quenches, as it were,

The grace of the Holy Spirit, God's own *kynde*.

    (17.271—2)

In this passage, see how many of these meanings of *kynde* and *unkyndenesse* fit in each line. How do the multiple meanings of "kind" and "unkindness" make the message richer?

Kynde=nature, kin, kind

Unkynde=the unkind, the unnatural

For what *kynde* does, *unkynde* undoes, as those cursed thieves,

Unkynde Christian men, for covetousness and envy

Slay a person, with mouth or with hands, for goods.

For what the Holy Spirit has to look after, those wicked people destroy,

Which is the living person and love, the flame of the human body.

    (17. 273—7)

And anyone who murders a good person, I think, by my understanding,

Extinguishes the dearest light that Our Lord loves.

    (17. 280—81)

In his old age when death comes near him, Will sees *Kynde* again. He is afraid and asks for help. *Kynde* counsels Will, "Learn to love."

We already know that one of the names for God is *Kynde*, and that this name means "nature" and is related to "kindness." Therefore, when *Kynde* tells Will to love he is telling him to do what is most natural and at the same time, most Godlike.

And as I sat in this sorrow, I saw how *Kynde* passed

And death drew near me. For dread I began to shake,

And cried to *Kynde*, "Save me from trouble!

Lo! How hoary old age has come to me;

Avenge me if it be your will, for I want to be away from here!"

"If you want to be avenged, go into Unity [the church]

And stay there until I send for you,

And see to it that you learn some craft before you come out."

"Counsel me, *Kynde*," I said, "what craft is best to learn?"

"Learn to love," said *Kynde* . . .

    (20.199—208)

Earlier we are told that *Kynde* created human beings "craftily." In what way is love a craft? How do we learn it? Why is it the "best craft to learn"?

Fourteenth-century English society tended to be anti-Semitic, even though few English people had ever met a Jewish person, since they had been exiled from England. Yet some people spoke of Jews as "companions of Judas," the betrayer of Christ. The poet is unusual in imagining the Jewish community as *kynde* and therefore more (*Kynde*) like God than unkind Christians are. Christian bishops who fail to care for the poor are "worse than Judas." He holds the kind Jewish community up as "teachers" for the Christian community.

No Christian creature would cry at the gate

Nor lack bread or soup if churchmen did as they should.

A Jew would not see a Jew go crying for need

For all the goods in this world if he could help it.

Alas that a Christian creature should be unkind to another

Since Jews, whom we judge to be Judas's companions,

All help one another with whatever they need.

Why won't we Christians be as kind with Christ's goods

As Jews, who are our teachers? Shame on us all!

The community for their unkindness, I fear, shall pay.

Bishops shall be blamed for the sake of beggars.

Anyone who gives an entertainer silver

And tells the beggar to go away because of his torn clothes

Is worse than Judas.

    (9. 80—92)

Why do we still tend to "give an entertainer silver" instead of caring for the poor?

Piers the Plowman
Enters the Story

How and where, in this poem, do we reach God?

The people have repented of their sins and want to find God, but do not know how.

A thousand people then rushed together

And cried upward to Christ and to his clean mother

To have grace to go to Truth . . .

But there was no one wise enough to know the way there.

[They] blustered out like beasts over valleys and hills

A long time, until it was late.

    (5. 510-515)

Have there been moments in your life, or in the life of your community or country, when no one seemed to know how to find the truth? What sort of guide would you expect and how would you know whether to trust him or her?

A character we have not seen before—not a churchman, scholar or king, but a plowman, a common working man—suddenly appears claiming to know Truth intimately. He is willing to lead the people to Truth.

"Peter!" said a plowman, and put forth his head,

"I know him as well as a student knows his books.

Conscience and good sense taught me his place

And caused me to promise him to serve him forever,

To sow and to plant, while I may work.

I have been his follower these forty winters—

I have sown his seed and attended his beasts,

Indoors and outdoors sought his profit.

I make ditches and I dig; I do what he says.

Sometimes I sow, and sometimes I thresh,

In tailor's craft, in tinker's craft, whatever Truth can devise,

I weave and I wind and do what Truth says.

For though I say it myself, I serve him to his satisfaction.

I have my pay from him well, and sometimes more.

He is the most prompt payer that poor people know:

He withholds pay from no one; they have it at evening.

He is as lowly as a lamb, and lovely of speech,

And if you want to know where he dwells,

I shall teach you the way right to his place."

    (5. 515—55)

What is Piers like?

The road to Truth which *Piers* describes may remind some readers of Bunyan's 17th-century *Pilgrim's Progress*. Each is a very simple allegory (a story in which every object and person stands for something else). In this case, the landscape is made up of the Ten Commandments and their opposites.

The poet suggests, among other things, that both "men and wives" need to be good-tempered, and that we need to avoid being bribed to lie about others, especially in court. Notice the money and fees that are there for the plucking.

You must go through Meekness, both men and wives,

Until you come into Conscience, so that Christ knows the truth

That you love our Lord God best of all things,

And then, next, you in no way hurt your neighbors

[But treat them] as you would like them to do to yourself. . . .

Then you will turn at a hill, "Bear no false witness,"

With a wood around it of money and many fees:

Look that you pluck no plant there, for peril of your soul.

    (5. 561—5, 580—82)

Piers tells the people that if they obey the Ten Commandments, they will come to a wonderful place which he describes here—a castle with a large household, representing a good Christian life.

Then shall you come to a castle as clear as the sun.

The moat is of Mercy around the manor,

And all the walls are of Understanding, to hold Wilfulness outside.

The battlements are of Christendom, to save human nature,

Buttressed with "Believe thus or you are not saved."

And all the houses are roofed, halls and chambers,

Not with lead, but with love and humble speech, as by siblings of one
   womb.

The bridge is of "Pray well; the better may you prosper."

Each pillar is of penance, of prayers to saints;

Of almsdeeds are the hooks that the gates hang on.

Grace is the name of the gatekeeper, a good man in truth;

His helper is called "Amend yourself"; many know him.

Tell him this password: "Truth knows the truth—

I performed the penance that the priest gave me

And am truly sorry for my sins and so shall I always be

When I think of them, even if I were the pope"

   (5. 585—600)

What do you think this castle really is? What does the password to the castle
mean: "Truth knows the truth . . . I am sorry for my sins"?

Grace is the gate keeper to the castle which opens a little gate into Truth's chamber. The surprise is that this chamber is in one's own heart. Truth is sitting there, comfortably, in his "chain of charity." The chain may be the love that binds him to us, or a decorative collar. In Truth's presence, we are to be like children, happy to relax with our father.

The poet warns that when we find God within our hearts, we must avoid pride and anger toward others. God will not leave our hearts, but we can be "driven out" from our own interior selves, and only God's kindness or grace will enable us to find Truth's chamber again.

And if Grace allows you to go in in this way

You shall see in yourself Truth sit in your heart

In a chain of charity, as if you were a child,

To let him be, and to say nothing against your father's will.

But beware then of "Get-angry," that wicked villain;

For he has envy to him that sits in your heart,

And pushes forth pride to praise yourself.

Boldness over your good actions then makes you blind

And so you will be driven out like dew, and the door closed,

Keyed and locked to keep you outside

Perhaps a hundred winters before you enter again.

Thus, to think much of yourself, you might lose his love

And get it again through grace, but through no other gift.

    (5.605—17)

Catherine of Siena, a contemporary of Langland's, speaks of entering the "cell of self-knowledge." Have you found ways to enter into your own heart? Do Piers' instructions fit with your experience?

Piers explains that the practice of virtue (presumably another way to talk about keeping the commandments) is a good way to enter the castle: being careful about our use of food and drink, being humble, chaste, kind, patient, peaceful, and generous. Habits of this kind are hard won, and without them, Piers says, it is difficult to get to Truth. A little comic interlude follows, as some of Piers' listeners can't imagine themselves developing these virtues. They are about to give up.

Piers' response is another beautiful surprise. God's mercy, he says, is more powerful than all the virtues, which, like the soul, are depicted as strong feminine presences.

But there are seven sisters who always serve Truth

And are porters over the side doors of the place.

One is called Abstinence, and Humility another;

Charity and Chastity are his chief maidens;

Patience and Peace help many people;

Generosity the lady lets many in—

She has helped a thousand out of the devil's pound.

And whoever is kin to these seven, so God help me,

Is wonderfully welcome and beautifully received.

But unless you are kin to some of these seven,

It is very hard, by my head, for any of you all

To get in at any gate, unless grace be the more!

"Now, by Christ," said the pickpocket, "I have no kin there."

"Nor I," said an entertainer with a monkey, "by all I know."

"God knows," said a woman, a wafer-seller, "if I knew this were true,

I'd never go a foot farther, for any friar's preaching."

"Yes," said Piers the Plowman, and urged them all to good,

"Mercy is a maiden there who has might over them all;

And she is kin to all the sinful, and her son, too,

And through the help of those two—(rely on no one else)—

You might get grace there, if you go in time."

    (5. 618-638)

What does it mean to you that Mercy is "kin to all the sinful"?

Sin, Contrition, Forgiveness

Piers Plowman is spiritually realistic. Its characters do evil and are distorted by it. Like the *Shewings* of the fourteenth-century mystic Julian of Norwich, this poem sees sin as a misery for the sinner as well as for others.

"So hard it is," said Haukyn, "to live and do sin.

Sin follows us always," said he, and grew sorrowful

And wept water with his eyes and bewailed the time

That ever he did deed that displeased dear God

  . . . and cried constantly for mercy.

    (14. 322—25; 331)

For in Latin, hypocrisy is likened to a dunghill

That would be covered over with snow, and snakes within.

    (15. 111—12)

Nothing hits so hard nor smells so foul

As Shame . . .

    (11. 434—5)

Like the Italian poet, Dante, Langland seems to see greed (covetousness, avarice) as the most dangerous and common of sins. He makes a comic picture of it weighing down and chaining priests who keep their promise of chastity but fall into sin through the love of money.

In another comic way of picturing sins, the poem imagines that we carry our sins (here, Flattery, Graft, Falseness) as horses carry riders: they burden us.

Many priests keep themselves pure in their bodies;

They are weighed down with greed, so they cannot creep out,

So hard has greed chained them.

And that is no truth of the Trinity, but treachery of hell.

(1. 195—8)

And Flattery fetched forth foals enough, then,

And set Graft upon a sheriff newly shod,

And False sat on a juror that trotted softly,

And Flattery on a flatterer elegantly dressed.

Then had the notaries no [horses]; they were annoyed

That Simony and Civil Law should [have to] walk.

But then Simony and Civil Law both swore

That summons-servers should be saddled and serve each of them.

(2. 163—70)

Do you think sin—the choice of evil—burdens us today, as individuals or as a society?

Sin is sickness, even though we choose it.

Why does God allow us to catch this sickness of sin?

To answer this question, the character called Repentance in this prayer recalls the church's prayer on the eve of Easter, which paradoxically calls sin a "happy fault," "happy" because our sins led God to become one of us. We were already created "in the image and likeness of God" and God was our father, but because of our sins, God's "son was sent to this earth / And became man." Because of this, God is now "our Father and our Brother," and if we abide in divine love, we abide in God.

So sin is a "happy fault" because it is the occasion for a new bond between sinful humans and God.

"Now, God," he said, "who of your goodness made the world,

And of naught made everything, and made humans most like yourself,

And then allowed humanity to sin, a sickness to us all,

And all for the best, as I believe, whatever the Book says,

O happy fault, O necessary sin of Adam!

For through that sin, Your Son was sent to this earth

And became man of a maid to save humankind;

And you made yourself with Your Son like us sinful people:

Let us make the human in our image and likeness; and elsewhere,

Whoever abides in charity, abides in God and God in him/her. . . .

You who are our Father and our Brother, be merciful to us."

    (5. 481—7b, 504)

What do you think it means to "abide in love," or to have divine love "abide in" you?

Awareness of one's own sins as sickness, burden, and distortion can lead to despair. Where are we to turn when we are caught in bad habits? How can we change? How can we learn to love? Early in the poem, a sinner comes very near to despair, but Repentance comforts him. He compares *all* sin, the sin of the whole world—wars, torture, betrayal, wholesale rape and pillage—to a glowing coal (hot, burning, painful, destructive). Yet when it is cast into the sea of God's mercy, it will be swallowed up, its fire quenched, its potential for harm lost.

The mystics speak of God, or the mercy of God, as a great sea. St. Catherine of Siena called God "the Sea Pacific," and St. Margaret Mary said that Jesus told her, "Sinners shall find in my heart the source and the infinite ocean of mercy."

Repentance says here, "Have mercy in your mind, and with your mouth ask for it." We are to welcome the sea of mercy into our minds, think about it, meditate on it, enter into it within ourselves, and continue to ask for it in prayer. We can jump into that sea, play and swim in it with great joy.

Then that villain fell into despair and would have hanged himself

If Repentance had not comforted him right away, in this manner:

"Have mercy in your mind, and beseech it with your mouth,

For his mercy is more than all his other works—

His mercy is over all his works . . .

And all the wickedness in this world that we might work or think

Is no more to the mercy of God than a burning coal in the midst of the sea

All sin is to the mercy of God as a spark is in the midst of the sea.

Therefore have mercy in your mind—and leave money behind!"

    (5. 279—285)

Think of the sea, or a great lake, as you have experienced it. What might "Repentance" mean when he says that divine mercy is like the sea? How can we have mercy in our minds as Repentance advises?

Will ponders the Gospel story of the thief on Calvary who asked Christ, when they were both dying, "Remember me when You come into Your kingdom." And Jesus said to him, "Truly I say to you, this day you shall be with me in paradise" (Luke 23:42-3). This story makes Will realize that, whatever one's sins, genuine sorrow for sin is always met with Divine Mercy.

On Good Friday, I find, a felon was saved

Who had lived all his life with lies and with theft;

And because he confessed his belief in Christ and confessed his sin to Christ,

He was saved sooner than Saint John the Baptist

And Adam or Isaiah or any of the prophets

Who had lain with Lucifer many long years.

A robber was ransomed sooner than any of them

Without any penance in purgatory, to perpetual bliss.

(10. 413—20)

Sorrow for sins is salvation of souls.

(5. 125)

How Do We Do Well?

Will and his friend Patience are hungry, and Conscience has Scripture bring them food and drink.

Throughout the poem, patience and poverty or lowliness are valued as "places" of grace. Both the literal poverty of poor people and the universal poverty of human frailty are hard, but are places where grace grows, a gift of the Spirit. We do not save ourselves, but in our poverty we must try to "live loyally and in holy life" depending on the Spirit.

Conscience very courteously then commanded Scripture
To bring bread to Patience and to me, his companion.
He set a sour loaf before us and said, "Do penance,"
And then he drew a drink for us, "Long suffering."

    (13. 46—9)

But grace is a grass, therefore, to reduce grievances.
But grace doesn't grow except among lowly people.
Patience and poverty is the place where it grows
And in people who live loyally and in holy life,
And through the gift of the Holy Spirit, as the Gospel tells:
The Spirit breathes where He will.

    (12. 59—63)

Do you have any experience of grace growing in your life?

Patience tells a working man, Haukyn, that God provides good food for all creatures, from worms to humans. He says that the best food for humans is the prayer "Thy will be done," which will give people strength in hunger, cold, or thirst, in prison or pain.

"No?" said Patience patiently, and out of his bag took

Foods of great power for all kinds of beasts,

And said, "Lo! here is food enough, if our faith be true,

For life was never lent without food being provided

To live by.

First, the wild worm under the wet earth,

Fish to live in the flood, and the cricket in the fire,

The curlew by nature in the air with the cleanest flesh of birds,

And beasts by grass and grain and green roots,

In meaning that humans might in the same way

Live through loyal belief and love, as God witnesses:

Whoever asks the Father in my name... and elsewhere, *People do not live by bread alone, but by every word that proceeds from the mouth of God."*

But I looked [to see] what food it was that Patience praised so

And it was a piece of the *Our Father—"Thy will be done."*

"Take this, Haukyn," said Patience, "and eat when you are hungry

Or when you are benumbed with cold or are shriveled with thirst;

And never shall handcuffs grieve you or the wrath of great lords,

Prison nor pain, for *the patient conquer.*

(14. 37—53)

What relationship is there between food that nourishes the body and food that nourishes the soul?

Conscience later offers Christians another food to keep them healthy—the eucharist, God's body, "as often as they have need." But he advises them that before receiving communion, they must pay all their debts, practice the virtues, forgive others, and then be absolved in the sacrament of penance. The people are shocked at this demand, but Conscience repeats it.

"Come," said Conscience, "you Christians, and dine,

You who have labored loyally all this Lenten time.

Here is bread blessed, and God's body thereunder.

Grace, through God's Word, gave Piers power,

The might to make it, for people to eat it

In help of their health once a month

Or as often as they should have need, those who have paid

To Piers the Plowman their debt, *Pay what you owe.*"

"What?" said all the people. "You counsel us to pay back

All that we owe anyone before we go to Communion?

"That is my counsel," said Conscience, "and [that of the] cardinal virtues;

Beforehand, each person forgive the others, as the *Our Father* demands,

"And forgive us our trespasses . . ."

And so be absolved and then receive Communion.

    (19. 387—99)

Why do we need to pay what we owe?

What is the connection in this passage between communion and community?

Holy Church tells Will to be moderate in fulfilling his desires and to "treat delicious drink with respect" because sometimes the body wants what is bad for the soul, and the soul sometimes rejoices in what leaves the body hungry. (What, for instance?)

"So, treat delicious drink with respect and you shall do better.

Moderation is a remedy, no matter how much you yearn.

Not everything is good for the spirit that the gut asks for,

Nor is everything that delights the soul food for the body."

(1. 34—7)

How is "moderation . . . a remedy?"

What is the difference between physical and spiritual hungers? Can one replace or usurp the other?

Speech and time are magnificent gifts: speech is "a sprout of grace, / And God's minstrel and a game of heaven . . . a fiddle." In our speech, we can tell God's story as a minstrel does, we can play with words to reveal their depth, and we can be a source of joy and grace to others.

A person does best who keeps himself by day and night

From wasting any speech or any time. . . .

Wasting of time, Truth knows the truth,

Is most hated on earth by them in heaven;

And next, wasting speech which is a sprout of grace

And God's minstrel and a game of heaven.

The faithful Father would never want his fiddle out of tune

Nor his minstrel a vagabond, a goer to taverns.

    (9. 97—104)

What do you think is a really good use of your time?

How does one "play" speech? Have you experienced speech that was beautiful like a fiddle's tune, engaging and instructive like a song, or fun like "a game of heaven"?

Langland valued education. We don't know where he studied as a boy—perhaps in the Benedictine priory at Great Malvern. He thought school was as close to heaven as we can come on earth, and that educating a child is giving that child a lifelong blessing.

He worried about the salvation of the pre-Christian philosophers, and even about the great Jewish philosopher-king, Solomon. He thought we should pray for them because we owe them so much.

For if heaven be on this earth, and ease to any soul,

It is in cloister or school . . .

    (10. 299—300)

Well may the child bless the person who set him to [read] books,

So that living according to what is written saved him, life and soul.
    (12. 186—7)

[Of] Aristotle, the great scholar . . . Of Socrates . . . [of] Solomon:

. . . God is so good, I hope that since He gave them the minds

To teach us people who wish to be saved

(And the better for their books), we are bound to pray

That God for his grace will give rest to their souls;

For educated people would still be ignorant if we didn't have the knowledge
    from their books.

    (12. 265, 268, 269—73)

How has schooling or reading benefited your life?

At one point in the poem, Will is overcome with fear about his own salvation. He is comforted by recalling Isaiah's invitation, *"O, all you who thirst, come to the waters,"* and imagines Christ as a nursing mother calling all of us, like infants, to drink the living water/milk of salvation at his breast.

. . . my heart trembled

And I went into perplexity and disputed with myself

Whether I was chosen or not chosen; I thought about Holy Church

That received me at the font as one of God's chosen.

For Christ called us all to come, if we would,

Saracens and schismatics, and so he did the Jews,

O all you who thirst, come . . .

And bade them suck a remedy for sin at his breast

And drink healing for evil, receive it whoever wished.

   (Isaias 55.1) (11.115—122)

In a period when Saracens, schismatics, and Jews were often thought of as enemies, Will thinks of them as part of the human family, all called to "drink healing for evil" if they wish. How do we think of people of other cultures and religions today? How can we and they "drink healing for evil" together?

Marriage is a way to Do Well, and it is meant to be as happy as "heaven on earth." The poet was against marrying for money or matching old with young. Instead, people should "Be married for love," and then be true to one another and work together.

True wedded living folk in this world are Do Well
For they must work and earn and sustain the world.

(9. 108—9)

And thus was wedlock designed and God himself made it.
It is heaven on earth. God himself was the witness.

(9. 117—18)

It is an uncomely match, by Christ! as I think,
To give a young girl to any feeble old man
Or to wed any widow for the wealth of her goods
Who shall never bear a child except in her arms!

(9. 162—5)

But maidens and young men, match yourselves together;
And widows and widowers, do the same.
Be married for love, not for lands,
And then you get the grace of God and goods enough to live with.

(9. 175—8)

Have you had experience of marriage as a source of grace?

The Poor and the Rich

Langland understood destitution. Perhaps he suffered it at times. He pleads with God to comfort the very poor who are treated so badly by society.

. . . beggars about midsummer sup without bread,

And yet winter is worse for them, for they walk with wet feet,

Very hungry and thirsty, and rebuked foully

And berated by rich people so that it is a pity to hear it.

Now, Lord, send them summer and some sort of joy,

Heaven after their going hence, who here have had such destitution.

    (14. 160—65)

But poor people, Lord, your prisoners in the pit of distress,

Comfort those creatures who suffer much misery

Through lack, through drought, all their days here,

Woe in winter time for lack of clothes

And in summer they seldom eat their fill.

Comfort your suffering ones, Christ, in your kingdom,

For how you comfort all creatures, scholars bear witness:

Turn to me and be saved. (*Isaiah 45:22*)

    (14. 174—180a)

Have you ever been destitute? How do you look at the homeless you see on the street, or respond if they speak to you?

Piers Plowman is very different from most works of its time because the author valued poor people and believed that we treat Christ the way we treat the poor. By "poor" he may have meant all people, since we all have the frailties and pains of human nature. But he certainly was especially aware of the destitute and of the injustices they suffer even through churchmen who talk about God but fail to imitate his mercy.

But the poor person may moan and cry out at the gate,

Terribly hungry and thirsty, and may quake from the cold.

There is no one to take him in, nor relieve his discomfort,

But they shout at him as if he were a dog and order him to go away.

Little does he love the Lord that loaned him all that bliss

Who in this way shares with the poor person . . .

If the poor didn't have more mercy than the rich,

Beggars might go to bed without anything to eat.

God is much in the mouths of these great masters,

But his mercy and his works are among the poor.

    (10. 58—67)

What can we learn from the poor today? Is our comfortable way of life just "loaned" to us as the poet says? Do we have an obligation to share it?

The next passage contains a promise and a warning. We often meet homeless people begging for food and work or sleeping in the streets. Often they are dirty, sometimes ragged, and we may find it hard to look at them. The poet believes that Jesus is disguised in these people, wearing their flesh and clothing and looking at us through their eyes.

People who work with the homeless say that when we pass them or are approached by them, we should look directly at them as we would at a friend, even if we have no money to give them. The poet's words suggest this when he says that Jesus is watching to see "where we look." If we look lovingly at the poor, he says, with a "kind heart," we will be seeing Jesus and expressing our love for him.

For our joy and our jewel, Jesus Christ of heaven,

In a poor man's clothing pursues us always

And looks upon us in their likeness, and with a lovely face,

To know by our kind heart and by where we look

Whether we love the lords here more than our Lord of bliss.

   (11. 184—8)

And in the apparel of a poor man and the likeness of a pilgrim,

Many times God has been met among needy people

Who never saw him in the clothing of the rich.

   (11.241—3)

Have you ever seen God in "a poor man's clothing"? Or "in the clothing of the rich"?

Rich people in Langland's time hired "fools" and minstrels or musicians to entertain them and their guests, and if the minstrels of the king visited a house, they were heartily welcomed. Here the poem recommends that the rich entertain "three kinds of minstrels"—a poor person or beggar to sit at their tables, a learned person to teach them about Jesus's sufferings, and a sick person to pray for them. All three come from God, and God will consider kindness to them as kindness to him. When the rich person becomes poor "in his dying," his treatment of these "worthy saints" will be his comfort.

Scholars and knights welcome the king's minstrels

And for love of their master, listen to them at feasts;

Much more, I think, rich people should

Have beggars before them, who are God's minstrels

As he says himself, St. John bears witness:

Who spurns you spurns me.

Therefore I advise you rich that when you have revels,

Have such minstrels, to solace your souls:

The poor person as a wise fool sitting at your table,

And a learned person to teach you what Our Lord suffered

To save your soul from Satan your enemy,

And to fiddle to you, without flattering, the story of Good Friday,

And a blind person as your jester, or a bedridden woman

To cry to our Lord for a great gift for you, to show your good praise.

These three kinds of minstrels make a person laugh

And do him great comfort in his dying

Because he listened to them and loved to hear them during his life.

These solace his soul until he himself be fallen

Into good hope because he acted thus among worthy saints.

    (13. 437—54)

Who are our fools and minstrels today? How do they "solace the soul"?

We normally see riches as assets and poverty as a liability. The poem teaches the opposite. Riches, it says, may hold a wealthy person back from heaven, or make it harder to get in where poverty and simplicity go easily. But a rich person who is true and merciful to others will find a "double" reward in heaven from the courteous Christ.

[There are] none sooner saved, nor firmer in their faith,

Than plowmen and shepherds and poor common laborers,

Shoemakers and shepherds—such uneducated people

Pierce with an "Our Father" the palace of heaven

And pass by purgatory without need of penance at their parting from here

Into the bliss of paradise, for their pure faith.

    (10. 459—64)

Often wealth obstructs the highway to heaven . . .

Where the poor person presses ahead, with a pack on his back . . .

Eagerly, as beggars do, and boldly he asks

A perpetual bliss because of his poverty and his patience.

    (14. 212—15)

. . . if you rich people have pity, and reward well the poor,

And live as the law teaches, doing as you should to all,

Christ of his courtesy shall comfort you at the last

And reward with double riches all who have merciful hearts.

    (14. 145—8)

What do "pity" and "merciful hearts" demand of the comfortable in the face of the suffering of the poor?

Langland believes that God's justice will comfort and reward the poor. Even beasts, he says, have the joy of summer after a hard winter.

[At death], the poor person dares to plead and prove by pure reason

That he should have an allowance of the Lord: by the law he claims it.

One who never had joy asks joy of a righteous judge.

And says, "Lo! birds and beasts who know no bliss,

And wild worms in the woods, you grieve them through winters

And make them nearly meek and mild for need,

And afterwards, you send them summer that is their sovereign joy

And bliss to all that exist, both wild and tame.

So beggars, like beasts, may expect something good

Who all their lives have lived in pain and in need.

Unless God sent them some time some sort of joy

Either here or elsewhere, nature would not stand for it.

    (14. 108—19)

Do you think that every creature has a natural right to joy?

The ultimate bond between the rich and the poor, for the poet, is kinship. We are blood-relations through Christ.

Almighty God could have made everyone rich if he had wanted to,

But it is for the best that some are rich and some are beggars and poor.

For we are all Christ's creatures, and rich from his treasury,

And kin as of one blood, beggars as well as earls,

For at Calvary, Christendom sprang from Christ's blood

And we became blood brothers and sisters, won from/by one body.
  (11.196-201)

Do you agree?

Three Lovely Persons

No one understands the central Christian mystery of the Trinity, but Langland loved to think and write about it, and to try to enable his readers to have some tiny understanding of it through faith.

The poem has many names for each of the three Persons, and compares them to a hand holding the entire universe "within them three."

The first has might and majesty, maker of all things:

Father is his proper name, a person by himself.

The second, of that Sire, is the Son, Truth,

Guardian of all who have intelligence, always without beginning.

The third is called the Holy Spirit, a person by himself,

The light of all that have life on land and water,

Comforter of creatures; of him comes all bliss.

    (16. 184—90)

And as the hand holds all things hard and fast

Through four fingers and a thumb with the palm,

Just so the Father and the Son and Holy Spirit the third

Hold all the wide world within them three—

The sky and the wind, water and earth,

Heaven and hell and all that is in them.

    (17. 157—62)

Today we sing the spiritual, "He's got the whole world in his hand." What does this image of God holding the world in his hand mean to you?

The Life of Christ

Jesus is called "Sun of Justice" in ancient Christian prayers. The poet plays upon "sun/son" in this retelling of the Gospel story of the annunciation from Luke 1:26—38.

God's decision to become human meant to the poet that a perfectly happy Person chose to learn sorrow, and an infinitely wealthy Person, creator of the universe, chose to become poor.

And then spoke the Holy Spirit in Gabriel's mouth

To a maiden called Mary, a meek person, moreover,

That one Jesus, a justice's Son, must rest in her chamber

Until the fullness of time had come.

    (16. 90—93)

And God left all his great spiritual joy

And came and took human nature and became needy.

So needy was he, as the book says, in many different places

That he said in his sorrow on the cross itself,

"Both fox and bird may fly or creep to a hole,

And the fish has a fin with which to swim to rest, but

Where need has taken me, I have to abide

And suffer sour sorrows which shall turn to joy."

So be not abashed to wait and to be needy,

Since he who made all the world was needy by his own will,

And no one ever died as needy as he, or poorer.

    (20. 40—50)

What is your definition of "need"? How is it significant to your life?

   The poem describes Christ's coming as a moment of lively action. The Holy
Spirit will *cleave* heaven open; Love will *leap* out of heaven; Cleanness, referring to
Mary, the Virgin, will *catch* Love; and scholars, the Magi, will *find* Love.

For the high Holy Spirit shall cleave heaven open,

And Love shall leap out then into this low earth,

And Cleanness shall catch it, and scholars shall find it.

    (12.140—142)

Do the words "cleave open" and "leap" suggest anything about the Spirit and Love?

Jesus comforted the sick and suffering during his life. Wearing our "armor," our flesh, he did the brave deeds narrated in the Gospels and chose to share our experience of dying.

He made the lame to leap and gave light to the blind

And fed with two fishes and with five loaves

Bitterly hungry people, more than five thousand.

Thus he comforted those burdened with cares.

    (19. 125—8)

And all that Mark has written, Matthew, John, and Luke

Of your bravest deeds were done in our armor:

The Word was made flesh, and dwelt among/in us. (John 1:14)

    (5. 500—501a)

So God who began all, of his good will,

Became man of a maiden to save human *kynde*

And let himself be sold, to see the sorrow of dying,

Which unknits all care and is the beginning of rest.

    (18. 211-214)

  Have you ever experienced "the sorrow of dying"? How has your experience of death shaped your life?

The Great Joust

As the poem reaches its climax, Will is discouraged and miserable. He sleeps until the beginning of Holy Week, and in his dream he sees the meaning of the events celebrated by the church during that time.

With wool next to my skin and with wet feet, I went forth

Like a thoughtless fellow who pays no attention to misery,

And went forth like a fool all my lifetime,

Until I grew weary of the world and wanted to sleep again

And leaned on Lent, and a long time I slept.

I rested there and snored until Palm Sunday.

Of youngsters and of *Glory and Praise* I dreamed a long time,

And how old folks sang *Hosanna* with the organ,

And of Christ's passion and suffering that reached the people.

    (18. 1-9)

Jesus comes riding on an ass into Jerusalem as the Gospel says, but it is a "modern" Jesus, a young man who comes to be dubbed a knight and joust with the devil. He looks like Piers the Plowman, for he is dressed in Piers' clothing, human nature.

One who looked like the Samaritan, and somewhat like Piers the Plowman,

Barefoot on an ass's back came galloping without boots,

Without spurs or spear; he looked lively,

Like a knight who comes to be dubbed,

To get himself gilt spurs on decorated shoes.

Then Faith was in a window, and cried, "Ah! the Son of David!"

As a herald of arms does when the adventurous come to joust.

Old Jews of Jerusalem sang for joy

Blessed is he who comes in the name of the Lord!

Then I asked Faith what all the fuss meant,

And who should joust in Jerusalem. "Jesus," he said,

"And he will fetch what the fiend claims, the fruit of Piers the Plowman."

"Is Piers in this place?" I said, and he gazed at me.

"This Jesus of his nobility will joust in Piers' armor,

In his helmet and in his coat of mail, human nature.

So that Christ will not be recognized here as the high God,

This horseman shall ride in the clothing of Piers the Plowman,

For no blow could hurt him in the Godhead of the Father."

    (18. 10-26)

Do you know anyone who has done battle with "a false sentence of Death"?

Jesus, like a medieval knight, is a hero who battles and "undoes" Death, turning the night of our grief and our death into day.

. . . Jesus was his name,

Who on the following Friday for the sake of humankind,

Jousted in Jerusalem, a joy to us all.

On the cross upon Calvary, Christ took the battle

Against death and the devil, and destroyed the might of both,

Died, and undid death, and made day of night.

    (16. 161—6)

How did Jesus "undo death"? Can we, too, arm ourselves against the presence of evil in the world and make "day of night"? How?

The poem's description of the actual death of Jesus is both touching and mysterious, leading us into some understanding of what Christians believe was really happening on Good Friday.

Like a young prisoner, pale and fainting, Jesus closes his eyes in death, but it is "the lord of life" who is dying, "the lord of . . . light" who closes his eyes. The whole world quakes at this death of God-man (as the poem calls him elsewhere), for it is the climax of the struggle between life and death.

"*It is finished,*" said Christ, and began to swoon,

Piteous and pale as a prisoner who dies;

The lord of life and of light then closed his eyes.

The day for dread withdrew and dark became the sun.

The wall quivered and split, and all the world quaked.

Dead men because of that din came out of deep graves,

And told why that tempest lasted so long a time.

"For a bitter battle," the dead body said;

"Life and Death in this darkness, each is destroying the other.

No one shall really know who shall have the mastery

Until Sunday about dawn," and sank with that to the earth.

Some said that he was God's Son who died so fair:

Truly, he was the son of God. (Matthew 27:54)

    (18. 57—68)

The Great Trial:
Who Can be Saved?

In the hours between Christ's death on Friday and his resurrection on Sunday, characters in Will's dream debate whether God can justly forgive sin, why God allowed sin, and why God became a man in Jesus.

Here, a character called Peace argues that only through knowing pain and sadness do humans fully appreciate and enjoy happiness. This, she says, is why God allowed Adam to sin, so that ultimately he would have joy. And "this folk" from before the time of Christ who were guilty of "folly and sin" and have suffered because of it will now know "bliss without end."

Peace explains that God, who loved Adam, undertook the great adventure of taking human nature in Jesus, so that God could experience all the sufferings of human nature. Unlike us, God already knew "all joy," but love drove him to experience our pain.

Therefore God of his goodness set the first man, Adam,

In solace and in sovereign mirth;

And then he allowed him to feel sin-sorrow

To know what good was, truly to know it.

And afterwards, God ventured himself and took Adam's nature

To know what he had suffered in three different places,

Both in heaven and on earth, and now he plans to go to hell,

To know what all woe is, he who knows all joy.

So it shall be for this folk; their folly and their sin

Shall teach them what suffering is, and bliss without end.

No one knows what war is where peace reigns,

Nor what is really good until taught by "alas!"

   (18.217—228)

And woe shall change into well-being at the last . . .

   (18. 203)

   Do we, like Christ, need to see heaven, earth and hell and to "know all woe" in order for "woe" to "change into well-being at the last"?

In Langland's day, Christians were deeply interested in the clause of the Creed which says "He descended into hell." Plays and stories imagine the ancient peoples imprisoned by the devil in a dark place and freed, after the Crucifixion, by Christ. The liturgy of Holy Saturday, Easter eve, recalls this even now, as a great candle is brought into a dark church and people sing, "Christ, our light." This passage from *Piers Plowman* dramatizes this church service. Everything is dark in hell, but the devils see "a soul . . . sailing toward us / With glory and with great light." The light *is* Christ, who challenges the devils, and with his breath breaks the gates of hell. The redeemed sing as Jesus draws those he loves "into his light."

And now I see where a soul comes sailing toward us

With glory and with great light—God it is, I know well! . . .

Again the light commanded them to unlock, and Lucifer answered, "*Who is
this?*"

What lord are you?" said Lucifer. The light then said,

"*The king of glory,*

The lord of might and of main and all kinds of powers,

The lord of hosts.

Dukes of this dim place, now undo these gates,

That Christ may come in, the Son of the King of heaven!"

And with that breath, hell broke open, with the bars of Belial,

Despite any person or guard, wide open the gates.

Patriarchs and prophets, *people in darkness,*

Sang Saint John's song, "*Behold the lamb of God!*"

Lucifer could not look, the light so blinded him.

And those that Our Lord loved, he drew into his light.

    (18. 306—7, 315—27)

Our lives sometimes seem enveloped in darkness. Have you ever experienced
being drawn into light at such a time?

Then Christ makes a great speech, as a lawyer might, in a trial, proving to his enemies, the devils, that he has a right to save the human race.

Therefore, soul shall make up for soul, and sin turn to sin,

And for all that humans have done wrong, I, a human, will satisfy. . . .

Now your guile begins to turn against you

And my grace to grow constantly greater and wider.

The bitterness that you have brewed, enjoy it yourself;

You who are doctor of death, drink what you have made!

For I, who am lord of life, love is my drink,

And for that drink today, I died upon earth.

    (18. 341—2, 362—7)

What "bitterness" has the devil, or Falseness, "brewed"? Why is he called "doctor of death"?

What does it mean for someone to die for love? Can you think of other heroes who have done this?

Christ's triumph is that his just power will rule and control all evil powers, and his mercy will rule all humans in heaven. He is a *kynde* king—kind and natural—whose kindness and whose very natures as God and man demand that he help his kin in their great need.

And then shall I . . .

. . . have out of hell all people's souls.

> (18. 372—3)

For to be merciful to humans then, my *kynde* demands it,

For we are blood relatives.

> (18. 376—7)

For blood may bear seeing blood hungry and cold,

But blood may not see blood bleed without having pity.

> (18. 395—6)

But my righteousness and right shall rule all hell,

And mercy all humankind before me in heaven.

For I would be an *unkynde* [unnatural, unkind] king unless I helped my kin—

And especially at such a need where help is so needed:

Enter not into judgement with your servant. (*Psalm 143:2*)

> (18. 397—400a)

What is the quality or value of mercy in your life?

Easter Morning

The whole universe rejoices, and Will and his family go to church to give thanks for Christ's victorious battle. It is Easter morning.

Many hundreds of angels harped and sang:

"Flesh sins, flesh purges sin; God, the flesh of God reigns."

Then Peace piped a note of poetry:

"Usually the sun is most brilliant after a cloud; and love is brighter after a
  quarrel.

"After sharpest showers," said Peace, "most beautiful is the sun;

There is no weather warmer than after watery clouds,

Nor no love dearer, nor friends more beloved,

Than after war and woe, when love and peace are masters.

There was never a war in this world, nor wickedness so keen,

That Love, if he wished, couldn't change to laughter,

And whose perils Peace couldn't end through patience."

  (18. 408—17)

. . . Till the day dawned, these damsels caroled

As people rang [bells] to the Resurrection—and right with that I waked

And called Kitte my wife and Calote my daughter,

"Arise and go reverence God's resurrection,

And creep to the cross on your knees, and kiss it for a jewel,

For God's blessed body it bore for our healing!"

  (18.428-431)

His Conscience teaches Will to recall the faith of Mary Magdalen and of Thomas the Apostle in their meetings with Jesus after he rose. Mary preaches the good news to everyone she meets, and Thomas, who had doubted the Resurrection, is invited actually to touch Christ's own heart through the wound in his side.

. . . Mary Magdalen met him by the way

Going toward Galilee in godhead and in manhood,

And alive and looking around—and she cried aloud

In each group where she came, *"Christ is risen!"*

Thus it came out that Christ overcame, recovered, and lived.

    (19.157-161)

Christ came in . . .

And took Thomas by the hand and taught him to touch

And feel with his fingers His fleshly heart;

Thomas touched it, and with his tongue said,

My Lord and my God! (John 20:28)

    (19.168, 170-172a)

And after his resurrection, *Redeemer* was his name,

And we his siblings, bought through him, both rich and poor.

Therefore let us love as dear children shall, and each one laugh with the other,

And from what each may spare, help where it is needed—

And everyone help the others, for we shall all go hence:

Each one bear the other's burden. (Galatians 6:2)

    (11. 206—210a)

How do you bear witness to what you believe?

The Holy Spirit Comes

Will goes to church and in his dream on Pentecost Sunday, fifty days after Easter, he understands what the songs and prayers of the liturgy mean: God's Holy Spirit, promised by Jesus, comes and gives people gifts. Piers here seems to be Peter, the head of the Christian community. The Spirit (Grace) says that these divine gifts will enable people to be good even in the face of temptation and corruption. The gifts of the Spirit seem to include all skills, talents, and kinds of occupation needed in the community.

. . . and then came, I thought

One Defender Spirit to Piers and his companions.

In likeness of a lightning he alighted on them all.

    (19. 201—3)

And then Grace went with *Piers Plowman*

And counselled him and Conscience to call together the community:

"For I will give today and share grace

With all sorts of creatures that have their five wits—

Treasure to live by to their lives' end . . .

And weapon to fight with when Antichrist assails you."

And he gave each person a grace to direct himself with

So that Idleness would not burden him, nor Envy, nor Pride:

There are diversities of graces. (1 Corinthians 12:4)

    (19.214—229a)

"Think that all crafts," said Grace, "come of my gift."

    (19.255)

What are your gifts? How were they given to you? How do they protect you? How do you use them to benefit others?

How the Story Ends

This story does not end, as Dante's does, with a vision of heaven or even of a perfect world. Instead, Will has to return to the real world, where corruption and violence almost overwhelm goodness, even in the church. Will watches Conscience set out on a new search for Piers the Plowman, who is out sowing God's seed, and who will be able to correct and purify society and the church. Will wakes up as Conscience's journey begins, and the poem is over.

The story is thus circular as perhaps the journeys of our lives may be. A search for truth is often followed by failure and falseness and then by repentance and a new search. Such a pattern is confusing and painful. But earlier searches in the poem have led to the discovery that Truth is always present in the heart and God is always seeking each person who searches for Truth, Grace, Kynde, or Love. So the poem ends in the mystery of hope that this new journey, too, will turn out to be a journey into love.

"By Christ!" said Conscience then, "I will become a pilgrim

And go as far as the world goes

To seek Piers the Plowman, so he will destroy Pride

And see that the friars have some income who flatter because of their destitution

And work against me, Conscience. Now *Kynde* avenge me

And send me favor and health until I have Piers the Plowman."

And then he called out for Grace until I woke up.

(20. 381—87)

AN AFTERWORD

The passages in this book can be useful to read not just once, but many times. For instance, you might read again:

—your favorite passages. Why do you like them? Do they articulate or answer questions you have? Do they speak to your own experience? Are they beautiful, so that you want to memorize them and speak them over and over?

—passages naming God in different ways and suggesting what God may be like or where God may be found.

—passages to help with fear, grief or sadness.

—advice on how to live a good life.

—passages for reflection on the life of Jesus.

—surprises you've found!

Then you may want to get a full translation of the poem and read it all, or tackle the parts you love best in the original Middle English, using the notes or a commentary to help you. Happy journey!

SOME TRANSLATIONS, ANNOTATED EDITIONS, AND COMMENTARIES ON *PIERS PLOWMAN*:

Attwater, Donald and Rachel. *The Book Concerning Piers the Plowman, Rendered into Modern English.* Everyman ed. London: J. M. Dent, 1907, 1957.

Bennett, J. A. W., ed. *Piers Plowman: the Prologue and Passus 1—VII of the B-Text.* Clarendon Medieval and Tudor Series. Oxford: Clarendon, 1972. [Middle English, with notes]

Covella, Francis Dolores, S. C., trans. *Piers Plowman: the A-Text. An Alliterative Verse Translation.* Binghamton: MRTS, 1992.

Donaldson, E. T. *Piers Plowman: an Alliterative Verse Translation, ed. E. D. Kirk and J. H. Anderson.* N. Y.: Norton, 1990.

Economou, George. *William Langland's Piers Plowman: the C-Version. A Verse Translation.* Philadelphia: University of Pennsylvania, 1996.

Goodridge, J. F. *Piers the Ploughman, Translated into Modern English.* Baltimore: Penguin, 1959, 1966.

Pearsall, Derek, ed. *Piers Plowman by William Langland: an Edition of the C-Text.* London: Edward Arnold, 1978. [Middle English, with notes]

The Penn Commentary on Piers Plowman. 5 vol. Pennsylvania U. Press, 2006—

Robertson, Elizabeth and Stephen H. A. Shepherd, eds. *Piers Plowman: a Norton Critical Edition.* (Donaldson transl. with Middle English text and critical essays). N.Y.: Norton, 2006.

Rose, Margaret. "The Ragged and the Rich: a Modern Interpretation of William Langland's *Piers the Plowman.*" Hastings: Pickpockets #26, 1996.

Salter, Elizabeth and Derek Pearsall, eds. *Piers Plowman.* York Medieval Texts. Evanston: Northwestern University Press, 1969. [B: selections in Middle English, with notes]

Schmidt, A. V. C., ed. *The Vision of Piers Plowman.* 2nd ed. Everyman. Vermont: Tuttle, 1995. [B-Text, Middle English, with notes. This edition is the basis of this volume.]

————. *Piers Plowman, a New Translation of the B-Text.* World's Classics. Oxford: Oxford University Press, 1992.

Skeat, W. W., ed. *The Vision of William Concerning Piers the Plowman, in Three Parallel Texts.* 2 vol. London: Oxford University Press, 1886, 1954. [Middle English, with notes in vol. 2]

————. *The Vision of Piers the Plowman by William Langland, Done into Modern English.* London: Chatto and Windus, 1931. [B: Passus 1—7].

Wells, Henry W. *The Vision of Piers Plowman Newly Rendered into Modern English.* N. Y.: Sheed and Ward, 1945.

Williams, Margaret, R. S. C. J. *Piers the Plowman. William Langland.* [B: translation]. N. Y.: Random House, 1971.

There are four versions of *Piers Plowman*, presumably written at different times of Langland's life. The shortest is called the Z-Text. The A-Text has eleven *passūs* (steps) or chapters. The B- and C-Texts both have a Prologue and twenty chapters though they are numbered differently.

CITATIONS OF BORROWINGS AND COINCIDENCES:

Prologue 1: coincides with Rose

6:          "enchantment," Skeat ed., glossary

8:          "hill," Bennett ed.

1. 34:   "treat with respect" Schmidt ed.

64:         coincides with Covella trans.

68:         "hinderer" Schmidt ed., Skeat ed., Salter and Pearsall

82:         "direct me to" Skeat ed.

145:        "believe" Schmidt ed. and trans.

169—70 coincides with Attwater, Donaldson, Economou, Skeat translations

5. 125   Skeat trans.

549   Skeat ed., Schmidt ed., Economou trans.

556-7   coincides with Covella trans.

576   "halt"   Skeat ed.

609   "Get-Angry" Schmidt ed.

616   "think much" Skeat ed.

634   "urged" Schmidt ed.

635, 638   coincides with Covella trans.

638   "in time" Skeat ed., Donaldson trans.

8. 48   "gives way" Skeat ed.

9. 27   coincides with Attwater trans.

31   "feature," "form" Skeat ed., Schmidt ed. and trans., Covella trans.

10. 299—399 coincides with Attwater trans.

11. 118—20 coincides with Attwater trans.

321, 326, 328—9 coincide with Attwater trans.

348   "If . . . it" Skeat ed.

364—6   coincides with Attwater trans.

12. 271   coincides with Economou trans.

13. 49   "long enduring," Skeat ed.

437—54   coincides largely with Economou trans.

14. 99—100   coincides with Attwater trans.

147—8   coincides with Attwater trans.

178   eat their "fill" Schmidt trans.

212   "obstructs" Schmidt ed.

324   coincides with Attwater, Donaldson, Williams translations

15. 111   coincides partly with Attwater trans.

218   "light of speech" Attwater trans.

17. 256—7   coincides with Attwater, Donaldson, Economou translations

271—2   coincides with Economou trans.

18. 21   "gazed" Skeat ed.

57   coincides with Rose

203   "well-being" Donaldson, Williams translations

221—6   coincides with Economou trans.

161a   Latin translation from Donaldson trans.

211—14   coincides with Economou trans.

366—7   coincides with Rose

409   Jill Mann's translation of the Latin

412—13, 414   coincides with Wells, Donaldson translations

19. 389—90, 392-3   coincide with Attwater and partly Donaldson, Williams, Economou translations

20. 40   "spiritual joy," Economou trans.

40—43   Economou trans.

SOME RECOMMENDED READINGS ON *PIERS PLOWMAN*:

Further bibliography may be found in the following studies and in the editions and translations listed above. For the latest articles and reviews of books about *Piers*, see the annual journal, *Yearbook of Langland Studies*.

*

Aers, David. *Community, Gender, and Individual Identity*. London: Routledge and Kegan Paul, 1988.

Alford, John, ed. *A Companion to Piers Plowman*. Berkeley: University of California, 1988.

Baldwin, Anna. *Guide to Piers Plowman*. Houndmills: Palgrave Macmillan, 2007.

Bloomfield, Morton. *Piers Plowman as a Fourteenth-Century Apocalypse*. New Brunswick: Rutgers, [1961].

Chambers, R. W. *Man's Unconquerable Mind*. London: Jonathan Cape, 1939.

Davlin, M. C. *The Place of God in Piers Plowman and Medieval Art*. Burlington: Ashgate, 2001.

Donaldson, E. T. *Piers Plowman: the C-Text and Its Poet*. Yale Studies in English 113. New Haven, 1949.

Dunning, Rev. T. P. *Piers Plowman: an Interpretation of the A-Text*. Dublin: Talbot, 1937; Oxford: Clarendon, 1980.

Frank, Robert. W. *Piers Plowman and the Scheme of Salvation*. Yale Studies in English 136. New Haven, 1957.

Julian of Norwich. *Showings*, trans. E. Colledge and J. Walsh. Classics of Western Spirituality. N. Y.: Paulist Press, 1978.

Lawlor, John. "Imaginative Unity of *Piers Plowman*" *Review of English Studies* 8 (1957): 113—45.

Muscatine, Charles. "*Piers Plowman*, Poetry of Crisis" in *Poetry and Crisis in the Age of Chaucer*. Notre Dame, IN: Notre Dame, 1972.

Pepler, Conrad, O. P. *The English Religious Heritage*. London: Blackfriars, 1958.

Salter, Elizabeth. *Piers Plowman: an Introduction*. Cambridge, Mass.: Harvard, 1962.

Scott, Anne M. *Piers Plowman and the Poor*. Dublin: Four Courts, 2004.

Simpson, James. *Piers Plowman: an Introduction to the B-Text*. N. Y.: Longmans, 1990.

Tavormina, M. T. *Kindly Similitude: Marriage and Family in Piers Plowman. Piers Plowman* Studies 11. Cambridge: D. S. Brewer, 1995.

Zeeman, Nicolette. *Piers Plowman and the Medieval Discourse of Desire*. Cambridge: Cambridge University Press, 2006.